"The pleasures of the table are common to all ages and ranks, to all countries and times; they not only harmonize with all the other pleasures, but outlast them, and remain to console us for their loss."

JEAN-ANTHELME BRILLAT-SAVARIN, in his
PHYSIOLOGIE DU GOUT, published 1825.

OTHER BOOKS:
The Terrace Times
    Minimum Effort Maximum Effect
Cook Book — Paddington Edition

The Terrace Times
    Minimum Effort Maximum Effect
Cook Book — The Rocks Edition

The Terrace Times
    Minumum Effort Maximum Effect
Cook Book — Balmain Edition

The Terrace Times
    Minimum Effort Maximum Effect
Cook Book — Looking at Cooking

The Terrace Times
    Minimum Effort Maximum Effect
Cook Book — Melbourne Edition

The Terrace Times
    Minimum Effort Maximum Effect
Cook Book — City of Sydney Edition

The Terrace Times
    Minimum Effort Maximum Effect
Garden Book — The Tiny Utopia

DEDICATED TO HOWARD
BECAUSE HE HAS DONE SO MUCH IN SO MANY WAYS
TO HELP MAKE THESE BOOKS SUCCESSFUL

1st printing October 1981

The Windmill in Wickham Terrace, on our
cover, is now known as the Observatory;
but it never functioned properly as a
windmill and was never an observatory!
It is, however, an important part of
Brisbane's history and one of only two
buildings left standing from the first
days of the Settlement.

Volume Seven
$5.95   Recommended Retail Price

The Terrace Times
COOK BOOK

BRISBANE
EDITION

Illustrations
by Reg Trebilco

Concept Text and Design
by Helen Arbib

INTRODUCTION

It is very exciting to be back with a new Terrace Times cook book. For two reasons.

Because it is the seventh in the series, which I never could have believed possible when I published the first one and thought it was the last one. Because, although it is the same light-hearted totally illogical mixture of history and minimum effort maximum effect cookery, it is set this time in Brisbane. I do hope Brisbane will like it.

I am sure everyone else will share my fascination with its history; it amazed me, as it did in Melbourne, how much I had to learn about a city just a short flight away. And I am equally sure you will all enjoy Reg Trebilco's illustrations. He was introduced to me by Jack Murphy of the New Central Galleries as an artist with the right light Terrace Times touch and interest in Australian history. He has had many successful exhibitions and is represented in business and private collections in Australia, America, Canada and England.

As usual, test-cooking and test-eating seem to take long enough to fill a vast volume, but only the recipes we like best are included. While they can never be typically Australian until we develop our own national cuisine, this time a number of Queenslanders have joined the ranks of family and friends everywhere who kindly share their favourites with us. I have marked them with a Q so you will recognise them, and have acknowledged the givers on Page 61.

You will see we now have a very simple Index on Pages 63 and 64, and the other books will each get one as they are reprinted. All the recipes are planned for 6-8 people.

Helen Arbib

THE TERRACE TIMES
15 ROSLYNDALE AVENUE WOOLLAHRA
NSW 2025 AUSTRALIA.

First published 1981.
Concept and text © by Helen Arbib 1981.
Illustrations © by Reg Trebilco 1981.
All rights reserved.
National Library of Australia card number and
ISBN 0 9598486 7 3.
Wholly designed and set up in Australia.
Typesetting by ASA Typesetting & Photography Sydney.
Printed by Macarthur Press Parramatta.

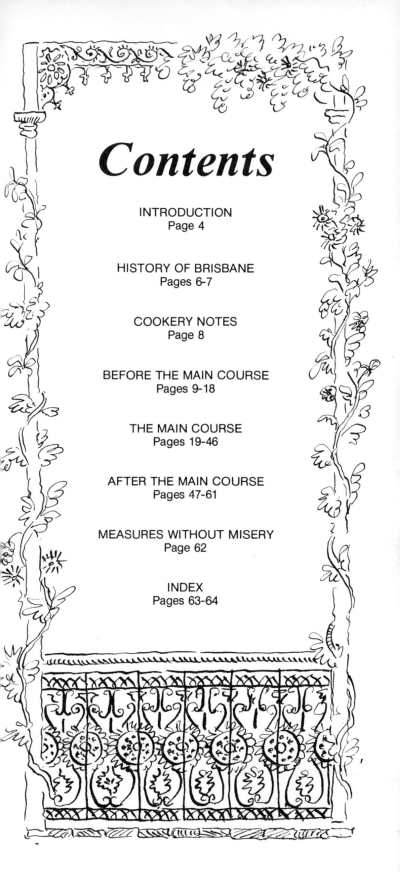

Contents

History of

Brisbane's history began, indirectly, when Captain James Cook sailed up the east coast of 'New Holland' in 1770 (18 years before the English flag was raised at Sydney Cove), glanced briefly at the bay he named for his patron the Earl of Morton, and noted in his journal that a river might flow into the bay.

In 1799, Lt. Matthew Flinders was commissioned by the New South Wales Government to explore the coast and Moreton Bay. But history began in earnest when, in 1823, Surveyor-General John Oxley was instructed to inspect the area, with others, with a view to establishing a new convict settlement. Sydney was overcrowded, no space was left at Norfolk Island, and Port Macquarie had proved too easy to escape from.

John Oxley found the river—with the help of Thomas Pamphlet and Richard Parsons who had found it first, after being shipwrecked—and named it for the Governor, Sir Thomas Brisbane. The new settlement was duly established at Red Cliff Point (Redcliffe) in September 1824, found unsuitable, abandoned, and re-established in February 1825 at what is now North Quay. Chief Justice Sir Francis Forbes wanted it called Edinglassie, after his Scottish home town, but Oxley insisted that it, too, be named for the Governor.

The Commandant was Lt. Henry Miller, who was paid 400 Spanish dollars for his first year with 29 convicts. His orders were to build huts for soldiers and convicts; erect a store, guardhouse and gaol; prepare 100 acres for growing maize; establish a signal station to warn of approaching sails; prevent the sale of spirituous liquors; and "take every opportunity of establishing friendly intercourse with the neighbouring blacks and punishing very severely any ill treatment of them." Solitary confinement with bread and water was advocated, rather than corporal punishment, and any corporal punishment that was given was to be supervised by him and not to exceed 50 lashes.

Such good intentions. But, instead, there was hardship and misery. The third Commandant, Capt. Patrick Logan, ran the settlement with "monstrous efficiency" and a high death rate, until his murder in 1830. Friendly relations between black men and white were rare, violence almost commonplace. The horrors of drought, malnutrition, poor hygiene and overcrowding, were added to the appalling difficulties of adapting to total isolation, in a strange environment, in a place nobody had even heard of before.

But the winds of change started to blow in 1839, when the penal settlement was officially closed. And again in 1842 when Moreton Bay was proclaimed "a squatting district" and the first allotments put up for sale.

Brisbane

Brisbane's first civilian was Andrew Petrie, who took up his Government appointment as Overseer of Works in 1837. The first free settlers were Lutheran missionaries, but the Aborigines refused to be converted and the missionaries turned to farming instead.

Like Sydney, Brisbane Town grew in haphazard fashion along waterways and bullock tracks, with Andrew Petrie's plans for broad thoroughfares frustrated by Governor Gipps, who insisted that narrow streets were best for a warm climate! There was, of course, an enormous amount to be done. Law and order to be established. The military garrison withdrawn. Communication effected between the settlements of North and South Brisbane. Roads and bridges built. Migrants brought in to ease the labour shortage. The first newspaper, the Moreton Bay Courier, was published in 1846. The first bank opened in 1850. In September 1859, Brisbane became a Municipality.

But the most important development came three months later. The people of Brisbane had felt ignored and neglected by the Government in the South and, after a series of public meetings, sent a petition to Queen Victoria requesting Separation. On June 6, 1859, the Queen was "pleased to erect the District of Moreton Bay, New South Wales, into a separate Colony to be called the Colony of Queensland." The excitement was tremendous … a public holiday was declared, flags were flown, cannons were fired, and fireworks lit the sky.

On December 10, 1859, 4,000 people lined the river banks at the Botanic Gardens to welcome their Governor, Sir George Ferguson Bowen. And a procession escorted his carriage to the home of Dr. William Hobbs, which was to do temporary duty as Government House and where Separation was proclaimed from the balcony.

The following years saw a Legislative Council elected. They saw Brisbane become one of Australia's most important waterways. Splendid public buildings were built, and villas with high ceilings and shady verandahs grew on stilts along the river banks and in the hills. There were floods, gold rushes, and economic crises. Railway networks were laid. Electric trams replaced Cobb & Co. coaches and carried millions of passengers at speeds of up to 15 m.p.h. Brisbane Grammar School opened in 1869. The Museum, the Art Gallery, the Public Library, were all established before the end of the 19th century.

In 1981, as we approach the end of the 20th century, only two stone buildings—the Old Government Store and the Observatory—remain to remind us of the remarkable beginnings of the City of Brisbane, capital of the flourishing State of Queensland.

COOKERY NOTES

I recently came to the conclusion that there are three main groups of cooks. The purists who insist on using only fresh ingredients and infinite time and patience. The people who cook because it is impossible to eat everything raw. And, finally, those of us who have discovered that cans and short-cuts and minimum effort recipes have affected our reputations as hosts and hostesses not one iota, but that we now have the time and energy to enjoy our own parties along with everyone else.

But minimum effort does not mean no effort at all. What it does mean is that the process of preparing delicious food can be simplified and streamlined in a number of ways.

It is not just a matter of using recipes as easy to read as they are to prepare.

*Cooking ahead wherever possible, the whole dish or part of it, eases last-minute pressures.

*Choosing dishes that look after themselves in the oven leaves time for those that don't.

*Having a second electric hotplate on low heat when boiling a saucepan on a high one, avoids waiting for it to cool before food is left to simmer.

*Chilling bowls and beaters along with ingredients for frozen creamy dishes, prevents over-beating and curdling the cream.

*Freezing cooked rice, lemon juice in ice-cube trays, packets of freshly chopped herbs, cup-size bags of fresh breadcrumbs, on quiet days, keeps them handy when time is short.

*Stopping worry about over-seasoning by going slow at first, adding more to taste at the end.

*Referring to Page 62 when inter-changing grams and ounces seems too much to bear.

Before the Main Course

*"When I tell my friends that we often eat Bandi-
coots, Kangaroo Rats, Wallaby and Paddymelon,
they look astonished, and yet there is no reason
why they should not be good for human food, as
they all live on grass or roots. Often a young bush
housekeeper is at her wits' end when killing-day is
postponed, and the beef has run out, little knowing
that she has materials for a sumptuous repast not
far from her kitchen."*
MRS. LANCE RAWSON,
QUEENSLAND COOKERY AND POULTRY BOOK, 1878.

Appetisers

I hate to hear anyone say they can't cook. Because, of course, what they are really saying is that they don't *want* to cook—and this means they are missing out on so much fun.

It takes a lot to beat the pleasure we get from preparing delicious food for the people we care about. And how much more so when maximum results can be achieved with minimum possible effort!

Oriental Ginger Dip.

Combine in serving bowl
    ½ cup sour cream
    ½ cup canned water chestnuts, chopped
    1 cup egg mayonnaise
    ¼ cup chopped shallots
    ¼ cup freshly chopped parsley
    2 cloves garlic, finely chopped
    1-2 tablespoons fresh ginger, to taste,
        finely chopped
    1 tablespoon soy sauce
    ½ teaspoon salt
Chill and serve with chilled raw vegetables.

Prune Tidbits can be cooked ahead, frozen, and reheated when required.

Soak for at least 1 hour
    250g packet pitted prunes, in
    2 cups hot teabag or strained tea
Drain. Dry. Fill each one with
    1 whole almond
Cut into 3 pieces
    rindless middle rashers bacon from 2 250g
        packs, allowing 1 piece per prune
Wrap around filled prunes. Secure with toothpick. Cook join-side down on large biscuit tray 10 minutes in 200C/400F oven. Serve immediately or freeze between layers of plastic wrap in sealed container. Thaw at room temperature 1 hour. Heat in 190C/375F oven 5 minutes.

Q **Egg and Avocado Pâté.**

Combine briefly in blender or processor
  1 from 2 avocados, weighing approx.
    210g each
  4 hard-boiled eggs
  2 tablespoons each lemon juice and
    mayonnaise
  1 clove garlic, crushed
  ½ teaspoon salt and ¼ teaspoon pepper
  1 tablespoon chopped parsley
  2 drops tabasco
Combine in mixing bowl with
  2 tablespoons whipped cream
  second avocado, diced and sprinkled with
  2 teaspoons lemon juice
Cover and chill in serving dish. Serve with
  lemon slices, parsley sprigs and toast fingers.

Crab Canapés. A handy not-really-a-recipe
idea to provide an instant appetiser for
unexpected guests ... provided of course, as
with any instant creation, the ingredients are
always on hand.

Combine in bowl
  1 170g can crab meat, drained
  ½ teaspoon dried chives
  ⅛ teaspoon dried onion flakes
  egg mayonnaise to make a smooth mixture
  salt and pepper to taste
Serve on small water biscuits. Or, better still, on
small bread squares quickly browned in butter
or oil, drained, and cooled on paper towelling.

Cheese and Nut Biscuits. It is the nuts, of
course, that make them unusual.

Crisp for 5 minutes in 180C/350F oven
  1 75g packet crushed mixed nuts
Blend well in mixing bowl with
  ⅓ cup soft butter or margarine
  1 cup flour
  125g mature Cheddar cheese, grated
  ¼ teaspoon tabasco and ⅓ teaspoon salt
Shape into approximately 36 small balls. Flatten
slightly on greased biscuit tray. Cook in
180C/350F oven 12-15 minutes or until golden.
Remove gently with spatula to cool on rack.

The reason why cashew nuts are not grown commerc
ally in Australia: they have poisonous shells which ca
only be removed by hand, so need to be produced
countries like Kenya and India where labour is cheap

Soups

Hot or cold, light or filling, soups are a wonderful start to a meal. And while nobody would—or could—argue the merits of using good home-made stock, making that stock involves a lot of time and effort. When there is none on hand, it's a joy to discover how well a few cubes and a little imagination can take its place.

Creamy Peanut Soup is unusual and delicious. I can't think of two better reasons for serving it.

Ahead of time, if you wish, cook and stir in large saucepan over low heat until soft but not brown
    1 inner stick celery, chopped
    1 medium carrot, chopped
    1 large onion, chopped, in
    2 tablespoons butter or margarine
Stir in and cook 1-2 minutes
    1½ tablespoons flour
Remove from heat and stir in
    2½ large chicken stock cubes, dissolved in
    5 cups hot water
    2 tablespoons whisky
    1 cup smooth peanut butter
Stir over medium heat until blended. Reduce heat and simmer, covered, 10 minutes. Strain into second saucepan. Purée vegetables in blender or processor with a little of the stock, then add to the remaining stock.
When required heat, but do not boil, with
    ⅔ cup each milk and cream
Serve garnished with paprika, and pass around
    a bowl of salted peanuts.
*The friends who test-ate this recipe argued a lot as to whether the added peanuts were a good idea or not ... but they all disappeared!

Lane Ciasto. Quick Polish noodles for soup.

Stir, little by little
    4-5 tablespoons flour into
    2 eggs well beaten with
    a pinch salt and pepper
Add only enough flour to make batter just thick enough to drop from a spoon in long streams into simmering soup. Cook 2-3 minutes, stirring once or twice to stop noodles sticking to pan.

"It has been said by a classical authority, that you may know whether you are going to have a good dinner by the soup which opens it."
THE EPICURE'S YEAR BOOK, 1868.

ST. PAUL'S PRESBYTERIAN CHURCH
Built of stone in Decorated Gothic style, St. Paul's stands on high ground overlooking Fortitude Valley on one side and Spring Hill on the other, and boasts one of the few church spires left in the city. Its foundation stone was laid in 1887 and the first sermon preached there in 1889.

Chilled sweet drinks look elegant when rims of the glasses have been dipped in beaten egg white, then in sugar, and left to dry.

Q Spinach Avocado Soup.

Combine in blender or processor
   1 cup raw spinach (silver beet), washed,
      chopped and firmly packed
   2 tomatoes, peeled and chopped
   pulp from 1 avocado
   2 tablespoons lemon juice
   1 clove garlic, crushed
   1 cup good chicken stock if possible,
      or 2 cubes dissolved in 1 cup water
   salt and white pepper to taste
Blend until smooth. Chill well and serve in small bowls garnished with
   chopped chives and parsley.

Instant Iced Tomato Soup.

At the last moment, combine thoroughly in blender or processor
   1 850ml can unsweetened tomato juice,
      chilled
   1 cup sour cream, chilled
   1 teaspoon seasoned salt
   a few careful drops tabasco,
      or 1-2 tablespoons brandy
Serve in chilled bowls, sprinkled with
   freshly chopped basil or chives.

A Very Special French Cheese Soup.

Strain into good-sized saucepan
   3 large chicken stock tablets, dissolved in
   5½ cups hot water
Bring to boil and add
   5 tablespoons risoni (rice-style pasta)
Reduce heat. Simmer 5 minutes or until cooked.
Combine in mixing bowl
   4 egg yolks, lightly beaten with fork
   ½ cup cream
Add slowly, stirring, 1 cup hot stock. Return to remaining stock. Reheat gently (it must not boil), stirring and adding a little at a time
   125g from 250g pack Swiss cheese, grated
Serve immediately and garnish each bowl with a very light sprinkle of
   freshly ground black pepper.

Emergency substitute for a glass of white wine in a recipe: a glass of water with 1 tablespoon white vinegar and 2 tablespoons sugar.

During the floods in the 1860s, thirsty Brisbane men were
known to row their boats to the bar of some local hotel
and be served their drinks while still sitting in them.

Curried Apple Soup. Hot or cold.

Cook on medium heat until soft and golden
   3 small white onions, finely chopped, in
   2½ tablespoons butter or margarine
Remove from heat and stir in
   1 tablespoon curry powder
   3 large chicken stock cubes, dissolved in
   5 cups hot water
   1 tablespoon arrowroot, dissolved in
   1 tablespoon cold water
Bring to boil, reduce heat and simmer 5 minutes.
Strain. Purée onions in blender or processor with
   2 medium eating apples, peeled, cored and
     chopped
   1 cup strained stock
Add to remaining stock and reheat. Stir ½ cup
hot soup gradually into
   3 egg yolks, blended with
   ¾ cup cream
Stir egg mixture into soup and add
   salt, pepper, and more curry powder to taste
Reheat without boiling. Or chill.
Serve each bowl garnished with
   1 very thin slice lemon, topped with
     a very light sprinkle of chopped parsley

Oyster Bisque.

Have handy a basin and large jug. In large
saucepan, halve and bring to boiling point in
their liquor
   1 large jar oysters
Pour into basin. Bring to boiling point
   1 large chicken stock cube, crumbled into
   1 cup cream and 3 cups milk, with
   1 bayleaf and a few sprigs parsley
Strain into jug. Sauté on medium heat until soft
   6 shallots, trimmed and finely chopped, in
   ⅓ cup butter or margarine
Add and cook, stirring, 2-3 minutes
   ⅓ cup flour
Remove from heat and slowly add jug liquid. Stir
over low heat until thickened. Add from basin
   oysters and liquid, with
   ¼ teaspoon tabasco and salt to taste
Reheat without boiling and serve garnished with
   chopped chives.

Salt was so precious in early Abyssinia and Tibet th
cakes of it were used as currency instead of coins.

Entrées

A Remarkably Simple Mousse.

Dry on paper towelling
  200g small peeled prawns (canned, if fresh
    not available)
Divide between 6-8 small pots or ramekins.
Combine in blender or processor
  1 430g can beef comsommé, less ½ cup for
    later
  125g packet cream cheese, sliced
  1 tablespoon medium-dry sherry
  ¼ teaspoon lemon pepper
Cover prawns, ¼-⅓ cup each. Chill until firm.
Then gently spoon on remaining consommé,
being careful not to disturb mousse. Chill again
to set. Garnish with
  tiny sprigs watercress or parsley.

Frozen Crab Mousseline rates high marks
as a summer entrée. It's cool and refreshing. It's
prepared in advance, always a joy in hot
unenergetic weather. It's easy. And it's different.

In small saucepan, stir over low heat 2 minutes
  2 tablespoons flour, blended into
  2 tablespoons melted butter or margarine
Remove from heat and add
  1¼ cups milk
Cook and stir until blended, then leave on very
low heat 5 minutes. Remove from heat. Stir in
  2 170g cans crab meat, drained
  1 envelope gelatine, dissolved in
  2 tablespoons hot water as packet instructions
  1 teaspoon salt and ½ teaspoon dry mustard
When cooled, fold in
  ¾ cup cream, beaten thick but not stiff
  ¼ cup light egg mayonnaise
  2-3 tablespoons freshly chopped parsley
Freeze, covered with foil, in ice cream tray.
Remove to refrigerator ½-1 hour before serving
(depending on how cold you wish it to be).
Unmould, slice, and arrange on lettuce leaves.

"Douglas Jerrold (English playwright) has said that such
is the British humour for dining and giving of dinners, that
if London were to be destroyed by an earthquake, the
Londoners would meet at a public dinner to consider the
subject."

MRS. ISABELLA BEETON, 1861.

Cheese is easiest to grate when just taken from the refrigerator.

Swiss Cheese and Pumpkin Casserole is a most effective party dish, as it is cooked and served in pumpkin. Ideal as an entrée for 6-8 or main dish for a smaller group.

Cut off top and remove seeds and pith from
    1 5kg pumpkin (easily done with soup spoon)
Toast on biscuit tray in 200C/400F oven 30 minutes or until lightly browned and crisp
    200g white bread without crusts, cubed
Fill pumpkin with alternate layers of
    toasted bread cubes
    250g Swiss cheese, grated
Press down slightly and pour on
    2 cups cream from 2 300ml cartons, combined
      with
    ½ teaspoon each salt and ground nutmeg
    ¼ teaspoon pepper
Replace pumpkin lid, place in shallow baking dish and cook in 200C/400F oven 1½ hours or until pumpkin flesh is cooked. Carefully transfer to heated platter.
Scoop out pumpkin to accompany each serve of cheese filling.

Easy Sweet-and-Sour Bread. It's easy because the beer provides the yeast!

Stir together in large bowl
    3 cups self-raising flour
    1 tablespoon dried onion flakes
    2 tablespoons sugar
    ½ teaspoon salt, followed by
    1 375ml can beer at room temperature
On no account must this be beaten or bread will become rubbery. Spoon into 1 large or 2 small greased loaf pans. Brush with
    2 teaspoons salad oil
Sprinkle with
    poppy seeds
Bake in 180C/350F oven 45 minutes or until golden and skewer comes out clean. Leave 5 minutes before turning out on rack to cool. Bread can be reheated briefly in foil before serving.

"In reproving the servants let it be done with tenderness, and never exaggerate their faults."
THE HOUSEKEEPER'S GUIDE, 1822.

The Main Course

"According to an unwritten code (still) well-known and honoured in the servants' hall, the servants who paid the bills received a percentage from the tradesmen of 1s. in the pound. The old newspapers and wax candle ends were the property of the butler, the lady's maid had the left-off garments of the mistress, the valet those of the master, the housemaid had oddments left in the bedrooms, the cook had the dripping, the kitchen-maid the grease, and the scullery-maid the bones."
    CASSELL'S HOUSEHOLD COOKERY, 19th century.

Fish and Poultry

Q **Seafood Supreme.**

Sauté in deep frypan until soft but not brown
  4 large shallots, chopped, in
  1 tablespoon butter or margarine
Cut into bite-sized pieces
  750g coral trout or other white fish fillets
Add to shallots with
  16 scallops chopped
  1 cup dry white wine
Simmer 5-6 minutes or until fish is just cooked.
Transfer to large casserole with slotted spoon,
saving liquid, and combine gently with
  4 crab sticks, sliced—
    if not available, use 170g can crab meat
  12 large king prawns, shelled, deveined and
    chopped
Strain cooking liquid into small saucepan. Add
  ¾ cup each milk and cream
Bring to boil and stir in
  2-3 tablespoons cornflour, dissolved in
    equal quantity cold milk
  salt and pepper to taste
Simmer, stirring, until lightly thickened. Pour
over fish and sprinkle with
  1 cup mild Cheddar cheese, grated
Top with
  1 cup fresh white breadcrumbs, combined
    with
  2 tablespoons melted butter or margarine
Cook, uncovered, in 180C/350F oven 20-30
minutes or until fish is heated through and
sauce is bubbly.

"It seems very strange to me that in this country Australia,
the land of sunshine and pleasant fruits, the sparkling
waters of her rocky coast and her swift-flowing rivers
teeming with fish, and yet her children living on a daily
diet of chops and steaks!"

MRS. H. WICKEN,
AUSTRALIAN TABLE DAINTIES, 1897.

Spicy Fish that looks and tastes very good.

Ahead of time, if you wish, sauté in frypan
   3 medium onions, finely chopped, and
   2 cloves garlic, crushed, in
   ¼ cup olive oil
When soft but not yet coloured, stir in
   3 tablespoons tomato paste
   1 bayleaf and 1 tablespoon paprika
   1 teaspoon salt and ¼ teaspoon pepper
   ¼ cup water
Cook gently, stirring, 3 minutes. Spread evenly over bottom of shallow ovenproof dish. Allowing approx. 225g per person, cut into serving-size pieces
   1.350kg-1.800kg cod or redfish fillets
Place skin-side down on onion mixture, in 2-3 layers if necessary. Sprinkle with
   2 tablespoons lemon juice
When required, cook covered in 200C/400F oven 45 minutes or until fish flakes easily (fish should never be overcooked). Serve in oven dish with
   chopped parsley garnish and a green salad.

Gemfish with Orange Sauce. In Spain this is made with fillets of sole, but the delicate and unusual flavour is the same.

Sauté approximately 4 minutes each side until cooked—they will have turned white
   1½kg gemfish fillets, cut into serving-size
     pieces, in
   2 tablespoons each olive oil and butter
Arrange on heated serving dish and keep hot.
Add to pan and sauté until soft but not coloured
   4 tablespoons finely chopped onion
Then stir in and simmer about 7 minutes
   ½ cup dry white wine
   1 cup fresh orange juice
   2 teaspoons finely grated orange rind
   1½ teaspoons salt
Pour over fish. Sprinkle with
   1 tablespoon finely chopped parsley
Serve immediately with mashed potato, to soak up unthickened sauce, and a green salad.

Easy guide to cooking fish any method: measure thickest
point and allow 10 minutes each 2½cm (1").

Smoked Mackerel Salad. A top favourite,
even though it is so quick and easy to prepare.
In large mixing bowl, combine
   2 approx. 400g Dutch hotsmoked mackerel
     (available from supermarkets), skinned,
     boned, and cut into small pieces
   2 inner sticks celery, chopped
   6 shallots, trimmed and chopped
   2 small turnips, peeled and cubed
   1 unpeeled cucumber, cubed
Combine gently with
   ¾-1 cup light egg mayonnaise
(The fish will flake but this does not matter).
Pile up high in a large bowl lined with
   leaves from 2 mignonette lettuces
Sprinkle lightly with paprika.

Q **Chicken with Green Peppercorn Sauce.** No
gourmet cook's reputation need ever be put at
risk with unexpected guests, so long as there
are barbecued chickens on sale nearby, to serve
with this superb sauce.

Halve and keep warm on hot serving dish
   2 barbecued chickens
For about 2½ cups sauce, heat gently together
   180g melted butter, with
   2 tablespoons lemon juice
   4 tablespoons from 175g can green pepper-
     corns in brine, rinsed and drained
Remove from heat. Combine
   4 egg yolks, with
   ½ cup cream
   4 tablespoons sour cream
   2 teaspoons French mustard
Add to peppercorn mixture and stir over low
heat until sauce thickens slightly, but do not
allow to boil. Add
   salt to taste
Pour over hot chicken halves and decorate with
   slices of avocado.

"Pluck a galah, put it into a pot with a smooth stone the
size of an egg. When the stone is soft, the galah is
cooked."
   AN OLD BUSHMAN'S RECIPE, TO DISCOURAGE
   QUESTIONS FROM CITY COOKS.

NEWSTEAD HOUSE, NEWSTEAD
The State's oldest remaining residence is now the headquarters of the Royal Historical Society of Queensland and open to the public. It was built in 1864 by the indefatigable Andrew Petrie on the banks of the Brisbane River and Breakfast Creek, for Patrick Leslie who was the first settler on the Darling Downs. Patrick Leslie sold it to his brother-in-law, Captain John

Clements Wickham, who came to Brisbane Town in 1845 to establish law and order as Police Magistrate. He later became Government Resident, until Separation and the appointment of a Governor. Until then, Newstead House was the centre of Brisbane's social life, and it is being continuously restored to recapture those gracious days in the lives of the privileged.

Chicken and Broccoli Surprise. But don't be deterred by the surprising mixture of ingredients; the end result is excellent.

Cook for half time specified on packet
    500g frozen broccoli
Drain, chop roughly, and combine in layers in casserole dish (broccoli first) with
    3 cups cooked chicken—most of a size 14 bird, skinned and roughly chopped
Combine well in a bowl
    1 440g can cream of mushroom soup
    1 cup egg mayonnaise
    1 tablespoon lemon juice
    ½ teaspoon curry powder
Pour over chicken layers and top with
    110g tasty Cheddar cheese, grated
Sprinkle over the cheese topping
    ½ cup fresh breadcrumbs, mixed with
    1 tablespoon melted butter or margarine
Bake uncovered in 180C/350F oven about 30 minutes or until heated through.

Lazy Chicken Breasts. Moist and tender hot or cold and, says the clever cook who gave me the recipe, "a great picnic trick" ... the foil around the chicken acts as a little plate.

Well ahead of time, allowing ½ per person, wash, dry, and remove excess fat from
    3-4 large chicken breasts, cut in half and left on bone
Place breasts in large bowl. Chop in blender or processor
    4 large cloves garlic, roughly sliced, with
    65g peeled fresh ginger, roughly sliced
Blend in
    6 tablespoons liquid honey
    8 tablespoons soy sauce
    8 drops tabasco
Pour over chicken. Rinse remains with
    juice of 1 lemon
Add to chicken. Leave at least 4 hours, turning occasionally. Lay skin-side up in baking pan on individual foil rectangles large enough to cover them. Top with marinade. Cover with foil. Cook 30 minutes. When required, cook covered 20 minutes more in 230C/450F oven and 15 minutes with foil opened up for skin to brown.

"*All* nice cooking—be its materials ever so simple—is more or less troublesome; but I have always found that bad cooks will take quite as much trouble to spoil food."
LADY BARKER,
THE PRINCIPLES OF COOKING, 1874.

UNITED SERVICE INSTITUTE, VICTORIA BARRACKS
*Built after the first barracks had become neglected and horrific,
the cannon bears the date 1865.*

Prue's Madras Chicken Curry. At its best
when cooked a day ahead.

Sauté in large heavy frypan until golden
    8 each chicken drumsticks and thighs,
       weighing together approx. 2½kg, in
    4 tablespoons ghee or unsalted butter
Transfer to large frameproof casserole.
Sauté in frypan
    3 medium onions, chopped
    3 cloves garlic, chopped
    3 granny smith apples, approx. 450g when
       peeled, cored and roughly chopped
    2 large bananas, peeled and sliced
When onions are soft, add to chicken with
slotted spoon. Stir into frypan
    3 tablespoons hot Madras curry powder
Fry 5 minutes, stirring occasionally, adding fat if
necessary so it does not burn.
Add curry to chicken mixture and blend in with
    4 cups chicken stock made with
       6 small cubes
    ⅓ cup raisins
    3 tablespoons pawpaw-and-mango chutney
    2 teaspoons fresh ginger, finely chopped,
       or 3 teaspoons ground ginger
    1-2 teaspoons cayenne, depending on how
       hot you like your curry
    1 teaspoon salt and ½ teaspoon black pepper
Simmer covered ¾ hour, uncovered ½ hour or
until chicken is tender and gravy thick.
Reheat when required and stir in
    juice of 1 lemon

GENERAL POST OFFICE, QUEEN STREET
The original building, the northern wing, stands on the site of the
'Female Factory', built in 1830 to house the few women convicts,
wives of convicts, and army servants. When they moved to
Eagle Farm, Andrew Petrie stayed there on his arrival as
Overseer of Works and the colony's first civilian. The GPO
opened in 1872 and, in 1892, typewriters were used for official
business in the telegraph office—for the first time in any
Australian city.

Meat

It always intrigues me that we have so many words in our vocabularies, so many more in the dictionary we never use, and all of them made from just 26 letters in the alphabet. It is equally extraordinary that, with a comparatively limited range of meat to choose from, we can create such a variety of interesting dishes ... with even more waiting to be discovered.

Lamb Tagine. A hot spicy stew from North Africa.

Have butcher cut into 2½cm (1") cubes
   1½kg lamb from leg
Ahead of time, if you wish, sauté until soft in a large frypan
   3 large onions, sliced, with
   3 cloves garlic, finely chopped, and
   1 large red capsicum, seeded and sliced, in
   3 tablespoons butter or margarine
Transfer to large flameproof casserole.
Fry lamb cubes, a few at a time and adding fat if necessary, until colour changes. Transfer each batch to onions with slotted spoon.
Heat in frypan, stirring
   1 teaspoon each ground cumin seed, chilies, allspice and whole coriander seeds
   1 teaspoon salt and ¼ teaspoon black pepper
Crush seeds slightly as they fry, and add
   3 beef cubes dissolved in 2 cups hot water
Stir into lamb and onions. Bring to boil. Cover and cook on low heat or in 170C/325F oven 1 hour or until meat is tender. While meat cooks, cover with hot water for 30 minutes or so
   60g each apricots and pitted prunes
   100g sultanas
Drain. About 30 minutes before serving, add to meat with
   1 425g can cooked dried chick peas
   1-2 tablespoons arrowroot, dissolved in equal quantity water if gravy needs thickening.
Reheat gently on stove or in oven.

"We trust the School Board will in time realise that it is at any rate as important for a girl to know how to make an Irish stew as to be capable of playing an Irish jig."
CASSELL'S DICTIONARY OF COOKERY, 19th CENTURY.

Roast Pork and Oranges.

Tuck under skin of
   2.25kg-3kg leg or loin pork, scored by butcher
   1 sprig fresh rosemary, if available
With or without it, rub scored skin with
   1 tablespoon oil and 1 teaspoon salt,
     for crisp crackling
   ¼ teaspoon black pepper
   ¼ teaspoon ground rosemary leaves
Place meat in baking dish in about 1¼cm (½") water (steam from water helps tenderise meat). Cook in 220C/425F oven 30 minutes, 2 hours with heat reduced to 180C/350F. Drain off about 80% of fat and water and surround meat with
   2 large unpeeled oranges, cut into eighths
Continue cooking 1 hour or until meat is tender and juices no longer run out when tested with a fork.
Arrange orange pieces attractively around meat on heated platter and keep hot.
For sauce, skim off remaining fat from pan and add to juices
   4 tablespoons dry sherry
   3 tablespoons redcurrant jelly
Mix well and cook on top of stove until liquid reduced to about 2 cups. Serve with meat, in jug or sauceboat.

Veal Aïllade from the South of France. But only for those who dearly love garlic.

A day ahead, if you wish, sauté until golden in large frypan
   1½kg lean veal, cut into approx. 2½cm (1")
     cubes
   2 medium onions, finely chopped
   15 cloves garlic, crushed, in
   ½ cup olive oil
Transfer to large ovenproof casserole. Stir in
   ¾ cup fresh white breadcrumbs
   ½ cup tomato paste
   1½ cups chicken stock made with 3 small
     cubes
   1½ cups dry white wine
   1 teaspoon salt and ¼ teaspoon black pepper
Cover and cook in 180C/350F oven 1 hour or until veal is tender. Cover, refrigerate and reheat. Or serve immediately topped with
   2 tablespoons grated lemon rind
   2 tablespoons freshly chopped parsley
To keep it company, boiled rice or noodles and a green salad. With parsley to follow ... it is said that chewing a few sprigs for a few minutes will suppress garlic's anti-social after-effects!

PARLIAMENT HOUSE, GEORGE AND ALICE STREETS
Queensland achieved Separation from New South Wales in 1859
and Parliament was opened by proclamation in 1860. Colonial
Architect Charles Tiffin won a 200 guinea prize for designing
what is regarded as Brisbane's finest building. It was completed
in 1891, when the Alice Street wing was added, but was officially
opened on August 4, 1868, so members of the Legislative Council
would no longer have to meet in the old convict barracks. In
those days, they were appointed first for five years, and then for
life.

Keep eyebrow tweezers in the kitchen to remove small fishbones. And scissors to cut herbs quickly for garnish.

An Amazing Pot Roast. So easy but so good. It can be made milder with less chili sauce.

Put in casserole dish
    1½kg piece of lean round or similar steak
Combine in a bowl
    1 small approx. 142ml bottle *mild* chili
        sauce, Malaysian if possible
    1 packet French onion soup
    1 375ml can beer
Pour over beef and cook, covered, in slow 125C/250F oven 1½ hours. Turn meat over and continue cooking 1-1½ hours or until just tender. Cool, remove from sauce and slice. Thicken sauce by reheating with
    1-2 tablespoons arrowroot, dissolved in
        equal quantity water
Return meat to casserole, cover with sauce and keep hot or reheat in 125C/250F oven.

Lamb-burgers. An interesting change from hamburgers, which originated on boats carrying German emigrants from Hamburg to America in the 1850s. The steak was salted to last the long voyage and tough, so onions and other available ingredients were minced with it to make it edible.

Ahead of time, sauté until soft and golden
    1 cup finely chopped onions, in
    3 tablespoons butter or margarine
Combine onions and fat thoroughly with
    1¼-1½kg finely minced lamb
    1 egg, lightly beaten with a fork
    ¼ teaspoon ground rosemary leaves
    1½ teaspoons salt and ¼ teaspoon pepper
    water if needed for a manageable mixture
Shape into 2cm (¾″) thick rounds, separate with foil, and refrigerate to set.
To cook, roll in flour and shake off excess.
Melt in large heavy pan
    1 tablespoon each oil and butter or margarine,
        or enough to just cover base of pan
Sauté burgers, a few at a time, on medium-high heat 3-5 minutes on each side until medium or well done. Keep warm on heated dish.
Top with a traditional gravy made with pan scrapings and wine, or with White Wine Sauce (Page 37).

"The chef who is a man of routine lacks courage. His drips away in mediocrity."
CHEF MARIE-ANTOINE CAREME, 1784-18

A Gourmet's Dictum: The host who has compelled a
guest to ask him for anything, is almost a dishonoured
man."

THE EPICURE'S YEAR BOOK, 1868.

Boiled Smoked Tongue is always popular
when it is served but, strangely, it is served very
seldom. Very good hot with Creole Sauce and
cold with Caper Sauce (Page 38). Or serve it as a
stunning sweet-and-sour party dish.

To remove excess salt and firm flesh, blanch
   1½kg smoked ox tongue, in
    cold water to cover
Bring to boil, simmer 10 minutes, partly covered.
Drain and plunge into cold water. Bring to boil
again in fresh water in large pan with
   1 large onion stuck with 4 cloves
   2 carrots, chopped
   1 stick celery, chopped
   8 peppercorns
Simmer, uncovered, 3 hours or until tender
when pierced with point of knife. When cooked,
skin will peel easily under running cold water.
Remove gristle. Cool in stock. Slice and simmer
in stock to serve hot.

Sweet-and-Sour Tongue.

Blanch, cook, cool and slice as above
   1½kg smoked ox tongue
Bring to boil in saucepan
   ⅔ cup pitted prunes, chopped, and
   ⅔ cup sultanas, topped with
   1 cup from 425ml can prune nectar
   2 cups water
Cover and simmer gently 30 minutes. Remove
from heat and stir in
   2½ tablespoons arrowroot, dissolved in
   ½ cup white vinegar, and
   ⅓ cup brown sugar
In large pan, sauté over medium heat until soft
   1 large onion, sliced
   1 large green capsicum, seeded and sliced, in
   3 tablespoons butter or margarine
Add prune mixture. Simmer, stirring constantly,
until sauce thickens. Add
   salt and pepper to taste
   tongue slices, spooning sauce over them
Heat very gently, partly covered, 30 minutes.

When freezing soups or casseroles, stand a plastic bag in
bowl or deep dish, fill, freeze, and remove from container
which can then go back into daily use.

UNIVERSITY OF QUEENSLAND, ST. LUCIA
*In spite of two Royal Commission reports dating back to the
1870s, that "the time had arrived" for a Queensland university to
be established, it was not until 1909 that the necessary Act was
passed. The University opened its doors in Old Government
House with three faculties—Arts, Science and Engineering. It
now has sixty departments at St. Lucia; a move made possible
by the generosity of Dr. J. O'Neil Mayne and his sister in 1930,
whose gift financed the purchase of 242 acres of land.*

49 LEICHHARDT STREET
This fairy-tale timber cottage in Spring Hill, built by John Fisher (circa 1864), has been restored and is used as a pottery gallery. An example of our belated but growing awareness of our responsibility to preserve the best of the past for the sake of future generations.

German Sweet-and-Sour Meatballs.

In a large flameproof casserole, combine
   6 beef cubes, dissolved in
   5 cups hot water
   12 ginger nut biscuits, broken up
Let stand for biscuits to soften.
In a large bowl combine
   1-1¼kg topside or similar minced steak
   1½ cups fresh breadcrumbs
   ½ cup plain flour
   2 medium onions, finely chopped
   1 teaspoon salt
   2 eggs
   water if needed for a manageable consistency
With wet hands shape into small balls, allowing 4-5 per person, and put aside. Reheat biscuit mixture. Stir well to blend, then add
   ⅔ cup brown sugar
   ⅓ cup lemon juice
   1 cup raisins
   1 teaspoon grated lemon peel
Stir over medium heat until sauce begins to thicken, remove two cupfuls, place meatballs in pan, and top with reserve sauce. Bring to boil, cover, and cook in 160C/320F oven 45 minutes or until meatballs are done.

Veal Gulyás. Gulyás is Hungarian for "cow-herd", so named because the original goulash was favoured by wandering cowherds, who cooked it over a wood fire wherever they happened to be.

Have butcher cut into 2½cm (1") cubes
  1½kg veal from shoulder
Ahead of time, if you wish, sauté in large flame-proof casserole on medium heat
  6 medium onions, roughly chopped
  2 large cloves garlic, finely chopped, in
  2 tablespoons margarine and
    1 tablespoon oil
When soft and golden add veal and cook, stirring occasionally, until no longer pink. Allow to simmer while stirring in
  1½ tablespoons paprika
  2 bay leaves
  1 teaspoon salt and ¼ teaspoon white pepper
  ¼ generous teaspoon each carraway seed, ground thyme and dried marjoram leaves
  2 large chicken stock cubes, crumbled
  1 425g can peeled tomatoes, roughly chopped in pan, with juice
  2 large red and green capsicums, seeded and thinly sliced
Top with
  500g field mushroms, roughly chopped
Cook, covered, in 150C/300F oven at least 2 hours or until meat is very tender. Add more salt to taste.
When required reheat without boiling with
  1-1¼ cups sour cream
Serve with large well-boiled potatoes, to be mashed into the gravy.

Baked Spareribs and Sauerkraut. Quite different from the usual ribs recipes.

Place in baking pan, allowing 2 per person
  12-16 pork spareribs, lean as possible
Roast, uncovered, in 200C/400F oven 30 minutes. Remove from pan and drain off fat.
Cover base of pan with
  1 825g can sauerkraut
Place spareribs on top and pour on
  1 small beef stock cube, dissolved in
  1 cup hot water
Sprinkle with
  1 teaspoon salt and ¼ teaspoon pepper
  ¼ teaspoon allspice
Cover with foil and bake in 180C/350F oven 1 hour or until ribs are well cooked.

Sauces

White Wine Sauce adds interest to most dishes without the problem of conflicting flavours.

For 1 cup sauce, sauté over medium heat
  2 shallots, finely chopped, in
  1½ tablespoons butter
When soft remove from heat and add
  1½ tablespoons flour
  ¼ teaspoon salt and ⅛ teaspoon pepper
Cook, stirring, until bubbly. Off heat, add
  1 cup dry white wine
Cook and stir on low heat until mixture thickens and raw wine taste disappears. Add more wine for a thinner sauce.

Tsatsiki, a Greek cucumber and yoghurt sauce to serve with lamb pilaf or curry, fried fish or fried vegetables.

Combine in serving dish or jug and chill well
  1 large cucumber, peeled, seeded and finely chopped
  2 cups natural yoghurt from 2 200g cartons
  2 cloves garlic, crushed
  ½ teaspoon salt and ⅛ teaspoon paprika
  3 teaspoons lemon juice
  1 tablespoon fresh mint, finely chopped.

"Do not lose your temper when anything burns through your carelessness; and never use bad language to the saucepans."
    EASY FRENCH COOKERY, CHEF AUGUST MARIO, 1910.

To keep a flour-based sauce warm, or reheat it, put pan
in which it is cooked into larger one of gently simmering
water to provide heat all around it.

Salsa Verde recipes vary a great deal. This
version needs no cooking, so the parsley stays
bright green, but it needs to ripen in refrigerator
for 1-2 days and keeps well after that.

For about 1 cup sauce (a little goes a long way)
combine in jar
　¾ cup finely chopped fresh parsley
　½ cup olive oil
　¼ cup tarragon or white vinegar
　2 whole cloves garlic, peeled
　6 capers, drained and chopped
　1 anchovy, drained and chopped
　⅛ teaspoon pepper.
Seal and refrigerate. Before serving remove
garlic and shake well.

Caper Sauce. Excellent with cold meats.

Combine and chill well
　1 cup from 250g jar prepared horseradish
　½ cup sour cream
　3 tablespoons drained capers, finely chopped
　½ teaspoon garlic salt
　1 tablespoon chopped parsley or chives.

Creole Sauce. Recommended, hot or cold,
with boiled tongue and with shellfish.

For about 3 cups sauce, half of which can be
frozen for another meal, lightly brown
　2 medium onions, chopped, with
　1 medium capsicum, seeded, chopped in
　2 tablespoons butter
Purée in blender or processor with
　1 440g can tomato soup
　1 small clove garlic
　¼ teaspoon each salt and pepper
Cook and stir over direct heat until boiling.

"In great cities in particular, how common is it that, for the
vanity of having a showy drawing-room to receive
company, the family are confined to a close back room,
where they have scarcely either air or light, the want of
which must materially prejudice their health."
THE HOUSEKEEPER'S GUIDE, 1822.

OLD GOVERNMENT STORE, WILLIAM STREET
One of Brisbane's two oldest buildings, it bears the crown of King George IV and its completion date of 1829. Intended as a Commissariat Store, it later housed convicts, the small windows barred against them getting in or out, the western doors sheathed in iron in case of onslaught during the 'bread or blood' riots of 1861. Its excellence was due to the expertise of the convicts who built it; the military had no such experience and buildings supervised by them usually had to be pulled down over and over again. The third storey was added in 1912.

OLD ST. STEPHEN'S, ELIZABETH STREET

Consecrated in 1850 and known as Pugin's Chapel after its eminent designer, it is the oldest church building in Brisbane and was the principal Roman Catholic church until the opening of St Stephen's Cathedral in 1874. It is said to be one of the finest Gothic structures in the world, which is not surprising; Augustus Welby Northmore Pugin was famous in England for his detail drawings for the Houses of Parliament, and for reviving Gothic architecture in England in the 19th century.

REG TREBILCO.

REC TREBILC

PETRIE TERRACE

One of Brisbane's few remaining terraces, lovingly restored. It stands in Petrie Terrace, which was named, with much of Brisbane, for the Petrie family ... Andrew the first Overseer of Works, his son John Brisbane's first Mayor. There was a gaol built there in 1860—its oldest prisoner, 96, was convicted of vagrancy; its youngest, 11, caught stealing fowls—but it was closed in 1879 when inmates were transferred to St. Helena Island. The Island has a number of interesting relics on display, from those prison days.

Vegetables

It's hard to vary the vegetables we buy. But at least we can vary the way we cook them.

Baked Lettuce, for instance.

Wash well, discarding only damaged outer leaves
　　1 very large or 2 medium lettuces
Blanch in plenty of boiling salted water 5 minutes. Drain. Press out as much water as possible. Chop roughly and fit tightly into buttered casserole dish. Top with
　　juice of ½ lemon
　　a light sprinkle of salt and pepper
　　a few small pieces butter or margarine
Cover and cook in 180C/350F oven 30 minutes. Serve with spoon and fork to drain off any liquid.

Or Baked Beetroot.

Place in casserole dish, with water covering the bottom
　　1 bunch young beetroot, washed but
　　　unpeeled and with some stalk left on
Cover and cook in 150C/300F oven 1-1½ hours or until skin can be removed with a finger; they must never be pierced. Cool and peel.
*Serve cold, sliced and sprinkled with a little olive oil, chopped parsley, salt and pepper.
*Serve hot, cubed, and reheated with butter and seasoning to taste.

"Steele's Liver Pills have done more to alleviate the sufferings of humanity than any other preparation science has yet produced."
　　　　20th CENTURY COOKERY BOOK,
　　CIVIL SERVICE STORE, BRISBANE, 1899.

"Boxing Day at South Brisbane.—A gratuitous dinner at McCabe's hotel had been given to all comers on the previous day, and to judge from appearances on 'Boxing Day' the host did not lose by his liberality."
MORETON BAY COURIER, DECEMBER 30, 1848.

Baked Corn on the Cob seems to have more flavour than when it is boiled.

Remove husks and wrap corn individually in lightly buttered pieces of foil. Bake in 230C/450F oven 20-30 minutes or until tender when pierced with tip of sharp knife.
*Serve as usual with butter and seasoning.

Sautéed Cucumbers.

Peel and cut cucumbers in 1¼cm (½") slices. Simmer in salted water, with a little vinegar, 5-10 minutes or until transparent. Drain well. Sauté in butter for another minute. Add salt and pepper to taste and serve very hot, topped with a sprinkling of
chopped chives or parsley.

Pawpaw as a Vegetable.

Cook green (not quite ripe) pawpaw as pumpkin, baked in the oven with a roast. Or steamed as marrow, served with a white sauce or melted butter.

Fried Capsicums.

In shallow pan or wok, heat over high heat
3 tablespoons vegetable oil
Stir in
6 large green capsicums, seeded and cut into thick slices
3 tablespoons soy sauce
2 teaspoons sugar
Cook and stir continuously, adding a little more oil if necessary, until capsicums are just crisp and serve immediately.

"Vegetables when not sufficiently cooked are known t be so exceedingly unwholesome and indigestible, tha the custom of serving them *crisp*, which means, in realit only half-boiled, should be altogether disregarded whe health is considered of more importance than fashion.
MODERN COOKERY, ELIZA ACTON, 185ᵉ

HAWTHORNE FERRY ON BRISBANE RIVER
The River has always been subject to flooding. Its first wooden bridge was destroyed by flood in 1869, and 1893 flood waters were eight feet deep in city streets. The gunboat Paluma, stranded in the Botanic Gardens, had to wait for the 1896 flood to refloat it back to the river!

Q Stuffed Butternut Pumpkin.

Two hours ahead, chop finely and soak
   100g each pitted prunes and apricots, in
   ⅓ cup rum, dry sherry or brandy
At cooking time, halve and scoop seeds from
   6-8 small butternut pumpkins (for 1 each)
      or 3-4 approx. 850g pumpkins (for ½ each)
Cut bases so they sit evenly. In saucepan heat
   40g from 80g butter or margarine
Add and cook until softened
   1 medium onion, chopped
   3 rashers bacon, chopped
Add and blend in
   2½ cups soft breadcrumbs or boiled rice
   soaked dried fruit and liquor
   ⅓ cup chopped parsley
   ½ teaspoon salt and ¼ teaspoon pepper
   2-3 tablespoons milk
Fill pumpkin shells. Arrange in 1-2 greased ovenproof dishes and dot with
   remaining butter or margarine
Bake, covered, in 190C/375F oven 1½-2 hours or until tender (if using 2 dishes alternate shelf positions after ¾ hour). Serve hot topped with
   chopped parsley.

Vegetable Pasta. Tasty, filling, and perfect after any outing when nobody feels like cooking. It can be prepared ahead, refrigerated, and popped into the oven when wanted.

In large heavy saucepan fry, stirring, until soft
    2 medium onions, chopped
    2 cloves garlic, chopped, in
    ½ cup olive or other oil
Stir in well to coat with oil and onions
    1 large or 2 small eggplants, approx. 500g,
        diced without peeling
    200g small mushrooms, roughly chopped
Cover. Simmer 10 minutes, stirring occasionally. Then add
    1 425g can peeled tomatoes, broken up in pan,
        with juice
    1 425g can tomato purée
    ⅓ cup freshly chopped parsley
    2 teaspoons each fresh or 1 teaspoon each
        dried oregano leaves and sweet basil leaves
    2 teaspoons salt and ¼ teaspoon pepper
Bring to boil. Reduce heat. Simmer 30 minutes covered, 5 minutes uncovered. While sauce cooks, boil as directed
    ¾ 500g pack lasagnette or similar long pasta
Drain. Rinse in cold water. Drain again.
Arrange ingredients in deep greased oven dish, about 23cm (9″) x 33cm (13″), in layers as follows, using approximate amounts
    ¼ cooked sauce, covered by
    ⅓ cooked pasta, dotted with
    ⅓ 400g ricotta cheese, topped with
    ⅓ 250 g mozzarella cheese, grated,
        sprinkled with
    ¼ 100g parmesan cheese
Repeat with two more layers, making sure there is a generous quarter of sauce to top final layer. Sprinkle with final quarter of parmesan. Cover and refrigerate. When required cook, uncovered, in 180C/350F oven 30-45 minutes or until hot and bubbly.

No wonder rabbits still run free. Under ideal conditions, a doe can produce 13 million descendants in 3 years.

46

After the Main Course

"The wages asked by servants is quite appalling ... fifteen shillings is the common wage asked by a general servant in Northern Queensland be she good bad or indifferent. If all mistresses would enter into a league and fix the wages at a certain sum, and no one gives over that sum, we might remedy the evil, and also get a better class of servant."

MRS. LANCE RAWSON,
QUEENSLAND COOKERY AND POULTRY BOOK, 1878.

Desserts

How strange it is that there are so many marvellous cooks who create the first part of a marvellous meal without any trauma whatsoever, then find the last course a perpetual worry and problem. Which is a pity, because a splendid meal is not really complete without a delectable dessert. And a delectable dessert can be among the easiest dishes of all to prepare.

Strawberry Magic, the ultimate in minimum effort maximum effect. And described by my brother-in-law, who gave it to me, as "75% air 100% delicious".

Combine all at once in large electric-beater bowl
    1 carton ripe strawberries, washed and hulled
    125g caster sugar
    2 egg whites
    3 teaspoons fresh lemon juice
That's all you do, except beat at half-speed at first, then at full speed for 4 minutes or so until bowl is about three-quarters full. Spoon into serving bowl, cover and freeze 3 hours or until firm ... then transfer to refrigerator, as too long in the freezer spoils it.

Spiced Oranges in Wine is an easy dessert that is ideal after a rich main course.

Allowing 1 per person, remove peel and pith from
    6-8 medium-to-large oranges
Cut into thin slices and remove seeds.
In saucepan, combine and bring to boil
    1 cup each sugar and water
    ½ cup each red and white wine
    1 small stick cinnamon and 3 cloves
    juice from ½ lemon, saving peel for later
Boil gently 5 minutes.
*For a hot dessert, strain liquid into second saucepan and reheat with orange slices.
*For a cold one, arrange oranges in heatproof dish, strain liquid over them, cover and chill.
*For both desserts, sprinkle oranges with
    2 tablespoons lemon peel cut into very thin strips, after pith has been removed.

English Almond Pudding is the perfect answer when time is running out, as it does not need lengthy cooking or chilling.

Have ready
  1 large sponge cake—a bought one for minimum effort
Combine in a small saucepan
  90g butter
  4 tablespoons caster sugar
  1½ tablespoons cream
  125g slivered almonds
  1 tablespoon cornflour
  4-5 drops almond essence
Cook, stirring, over medium heat until mixture bubbles. Spread over sponge cake, with almonds evenly distributed. Cover with inverted plate. About 15 minutes before serving, place in 190C/380F oven until cake is hot and almonds lightly browned.

Q **Ginger Soufflé.**

Beat together until pale and thick
  6 egg yolks
  ½ cup caster sugar
  1 teaspoon ground ginger
Heat milk until lukewarm and pour into egg mixture gradually, stirring well. Transfer to top of double boiler and stir until it coats back of spoon. Cool slightly, then stir in
  6 teaspoons gelatine that have been dissolved over hot water in
  ½ cup plus 1 tablespoon green ginger wine
Transfer to mixing bowl. Refrigerate until thick and heavy, but not yet set. Fold in
  ⅔ cup cream, whipped thick, and
  2 tablespoons chopped crystallised ginger, followed by
  6 egg whites, beaten stiff
Spoon into deep glass bowl. Chill until set.
Serve topped with
  swirl of extra whipped cream and chopped ginger

ORMISTON HOUSE, ORMISTON VILLAGE
Considered one of the best examples of early colonial architecture, Ormiston House was built by the Honourable Louis Hope,
seventh son of the Earl of Hopetoun, with cedar grown in the
local rain forests. Captain Hope is remembered as the father of
Queensland's sugar cane industry, and for the sugar mill built in
the grounds of the house after John Buhot had produced the first
five pounds of granulated sugar—from seven gallons of liquor,
and cane grown in the Botanical Gardens. Millions of tonnes of
sugar have been produced in Queensland since that exciting day
in 1862.

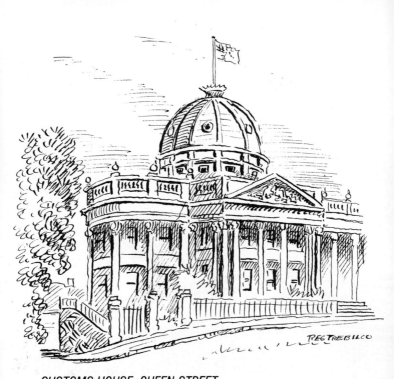

CUSTOMS HOUSE, QUEEN STREET
The first Customs House opened in 1850 when Brisbane won its battle with Ipswich and Cleveland to be the capital and main commercial port. Today's building, completed in 1889, is noted for its copper dome and position on the river bank. Although the interior was gutted and modernised in 1950, not one detail of the exterior was allowed to be changed.

Mousse au Chocolat from a New York cousin. "It's excellent, extra fast, and gives you a delicious feeling of sin," she writes, "but with no added sugar, no flour, butter or cream, it has less calories than most other desserts. And, refrigerated one day ahead, it tastes like heaven!"

Have ready, allowing 1 per person
  6-8 egg whites, beaten thick and stiff
Melt, stirring constantly on very low heat or in double boiler, allowing approx. 28g per person
  170g-225g cooking chocolate
  2-3 teaspoons water
Transfer to mixing bowl and beat in
  6-8 egg yolks, one at a time
Fold in beaten whites. Spoon into long-stemmed champagne glasses, or elegant glass bowl, and chill.
*Incidentally, the first chocolate mousse is said to have been invented in Paris by Toulouse-Lautrec. He called it chocolate mayonnaise.

52

I am not including recipes for fresh tropical fruits, such as mangoes and pineapples. I believe they should be treated with respect and served as simply as possible ... just moistened with cointreau or kirsch—or, if you prefer, lemon or lime juice—and chilled.

For creamy desserts, it is quite as effective *and* far more economical to use canned fruits.

Mango Fool is one simple example.

Purée in bowl
  2 430g can sliced mangoes, well drained
Combine the purée with
  1 300ml carton cream, beaten thick
  caster sugar to taste
Spoon into 6-8 small glasses. Cover and chill. Serve sprinkled with
  ground nutmeg or ginger.

Pineapple Marshmallow is another.

Drain thoroughly
  1 450g can crushed pineapple in syrup
Combine with
  1 100g packet white marshmallows, cut small
    (it's easiest with scissors)
  1 cup cream, lightly thickened with
    a pinch of salt
  1 tablespoon brandy
Sprinkle very lightly with
  desiccated coconut
Cover. Chill. Serve in 6-8 small pots or dishes as, like the Mango Fool, it's very rich.

Q **Green Grape Special**.

Combine in large glass jar, allowing approx. 90g per person
    550g-720g green seedless grapes, washed,
      dried and destalked, with a marinade of
    ½ cup each liquid honey and brandy
    2 tablespoons lemon juice
Refrigerate at least 4-5 hours, shaking jar occasionally so all grapes are marinaded. Just before serving, spoon into 6-8 chilled brandy glasses or small glass dishes. Top with marinade. Cover lightly with
  liquid cream from 300ml carton
Dust cream with
  a very little ground cinnamon.

Passion! Goodness knows how it got its name; the original recipe did not even include passionfruit.

Beat until thick but not stiff
  1 300ml carton cream
Fold into it
  1½ 200g cartons natural yoghurt
  pulp of 4 large passionfruit
Spoon into small pots and sprinkle lightly with light brown sugar.
Refrigerate, uncovered, overnight. Before serving, add just a little more sugar.

Q **Macadamia Nut Ice Cream.**

A day ahead, soften slightly at room temperature
  2 litre pack favourite vanilla ice cream
Melt in very small saucepan over medium heat
  65g unsalted butter
Before it browns, stir into it
  3 tablespoons sugar
Continue stirring 4-5 minutes until sugar caramelizes. Add to caramel and any butter separated from it, coating them thoroughly
    150g unsalted macadamia nuts, roughly
      chopped (if salted, rub off as much as
      possible)
Cool on greaseproof paper. Separate nuts stuck together. Save a few for garnish and stir the rest into softened ice cream with
  1 tablespoon brown rum
Freeze overnight, covered, in serving bowl.

Quick Fruit Pudding from Canada.

Mix together in bowl
  ⅓ cup brown sugar
  1 cup plain flour
  2 teaspoons baking powder
  ½ teaspoon salt
  ½ cup each raisins and sultanas
Mix and heat in a saucepan until sugar melts
  3 teaspoons butter or margarine
  ½ cup brown sugar and
  1 cup water
Pour into shallow 20cm (8") circular ovenproof serving dish. Drop in dessertspoonfuls of fruit-flour mixture. Cook, uncovered and unstirred, in 190C/375F oven 40 minutes or until golden and a knife comes out clean. Serve hot with
  whipped cream or vanilla ice cream.

Ice Cream Cake. A recipe that evolved years ago when I got bored making traditional birthday cakes, it is now a dessert that creates a sensation each time I serve it.

About 30 minutes ahead of time, chill in freezer
    1 410g can evaporated milk
    1 300ml carton cream
    large bowl, beater, 2 small bowls
And leave to cool in a cup
    2½ tablespoons drinking chocolate and
    1 teaspoon instant coffee, dissolved in
    3 teaspoons boiling water
In large chilled bowl, beat on high speed until very thick
    evaporated milk with a pinch of salt
Reduce speed and blend in little by little
    ¾ cup cream, followed by
    6 tablespoons caster sugar
    4 drops vanilla essence
Spoon approx. one third mixture into each small bowl; refrigerate. Stir into mixture remaining in large bowl
    1 30g flaked chocolate, crumbled,
      or grated chocolate
Spoon onto base of 20cm (8″) springform tin. Stir into one small bowl of mixture
    1 tablespoon strawberry jam
    2-3 careful drops red food colour
Spoon onto vanilla mixture in tin; don't worry if it sinks a little. Add cooled drinking chocolate to final small bowl of mixture, spoon into tin, and cover the three layers completely with
    remaining cream, beaten thick and
    sweetened with
    2 tablespoons caster sugar
Swirl with fork. Freeze, covered, 3 hours or until firm. About 30 minutes before serving, remove springform surround, leaving cake on base, and place on serving platter in refrigerator.

Special Steamed Rhubarb. Cooked without water, it keeps its colour, all its flavour, and makes its own juice.

Place in top of a double boiler
    1 bunch rhubarb, washed, trimmed, chopped,
      and mixed with
    ¼ cup sugar to each cup chopped fruit
Cover and steam, *unstirred*, over simmering water until tender. Serve with cream or custard.

ADELAIDE HOUSE (THE DEANERY), ANN STREET
Built by Andrew Petrie for Dr. William Hobbs, a remarkable man
who was brought to Brisbane in 1849 by Dr. John Dunmore Lang,
whose aim it was to populate the colony with "virtuous"
Presbyterians from Britain! William Hobbs established a farm
for dugongs (herbivorous sea mammals) to produce a substitute for cod liver oil, pioneered malarial mosquito research, and

REX TREBILCO

gave Queensland's first anaesthetic. The house is no less interesting. It was rented for the first Governor, Sir George Ferguson Bowen, until Government House could be built, and the new colony was proclaimed from its balcony on December 10, 1859. Dr. Hobbs sold the house to the Church of England when the Council decided to put Adelaide Street through his front garden, and it became The Deanery.

A new taste idea from Trinidad: orange segments dusted
with salt, and strawberries lightly peppered.

Q **Custard Apple Mousse** is so luscious and
unusual it's worth ignoring the fact that seeding
custard apples is not exactly minimum effort!

Peel and seed
    1 large and 1 small custard apple, to weigh
       approx. 365g without peel and seeds
Purée in blender or processor. Transfer to
mixing bowl. Add
    2 teaspoons gelatine, dissolved in
    1½ tablespoons hot water as packet
       instructions
    1 tablespoon lemon juice
    1½ tablespoons sugar
Fold in
    1 egg white, stiffly beaten
    1 300ml carton cream, beaten until thick
Spoon into 6-8 individual dishes or one large
one. Chill for at least 4 hours.

    Coffee Pavlova, a variation of the famous
sweet created by a Perth hotel chef in 1935, to
honour visiting ballerina Anna Pavlova.

In mixing bowl, slowly add
    250g caster sugar, to
    4 egg whites that have been beaten very stiff
Beat 2 minutes longer with
    1 teaspoon each cornflour and white vinegar
    1 tablespoon instant coffee
    pinch of cream of tartar
Pile onto greased foil-lined biscuit tray. Shape
into round. Cook 5 minutes in 190C/375F oven,
1 hour more with heat turned back to
125C/250F.
Cool. Remove carefully to platter. Top with
    whipped cream, sweetened to taste
    a sprinkling of slivered almonds, lightly
       toasted in oven after removing pavlova
    grated chocolate.

REG TREBILCO

MOONEY MEMORIAL FOUNTAIN, EAGLE STREET
In the early 1860s and for many years after that, most of Brisbane's buildings were wooden ones, and it was not unusual for whole blocks of Queen Street shops to be totally destroyed by fire. In 1877, a Queen Street grocery warehouse went up in flames, and little could be done to save it as the reservoir water had been turned off for the weekend. James Mooney, a young American volunteer fireman with the City Brigade, died as a result of burns at that fire, and the Mooney Fountain was built by public subscription in his memory. It has often been noted, however, that while the names of the mayor and aldermen are included in the inscription, no mention is made of James Mooney!

Tea and Coffee

It was British Prime Minister William Gladstone who said: "If you are cold, tea will warm you; if you are too heated, it will cool you; if you are depressed, it will cheer you; if you are excited, it will calm you."

Most Australians would agree. Putting on the kettle for a cuppa seems to be our automatic response to any situation. But that cannot change the fact that—for me, at least—tea will never be a satisfactory substitute for after-dinner coffee.

Sitting round the table, too content to want to leave it, isn't the same without a pot of coffee adding the final touch to that special glow created by good food and wine, pleasant company, and stimulating conversation. And then only when it is 'real' coffee; there's no magic in instant!

I suppose it's the commercial emphasis on instant coffee that tends to prevent us from discovering how much nicer it is, and how easy, to make the other kind ... heating the pot ... putting in 1 heaped dessertspoonful for each cup ... adding boiling water ... stirring, covering, and standing 3 minutes ... then straining it, or settling the grounds with a few drops of cold water sprinkled on top. But there are many other ways of making coffee, which originated all over the world.

Kopi Tubruk comes to us from Indonesia.
Put 2 teaspoons freshly ground coffee (medium-grind is best) in a glass, with white sugar to taste. Add a metal spoon to stop it cracking, and pour on boiling water. Stir slowly to mix coffee with water and sugar. Then leave a few minutes to let the grounds settle.

Ahweh, Lebanese coffee, is traditionally made in a *rakweh*, a metal pot with a long handle, but a small saucepan will do.
Allow for each small cup, 1 cup cold water with 1-1½ teaspoons sugar. Bring to boil, stirring. Add 1 heaped teaspoon very finely ground, or Turkish powdered, coffee. Bring to boil again over a brisk heat, removing it as it froths up. When the froth has subsided, repeat the process 3 times. Pour a little at a time into each cup, to divide coffee, sediment and froth between them.

In East Africa, coffee drinkers sweeten the brew by putting a dab of honey under their tongue and letting it melt into each hot mouthful.

Chocolate Strawberries. Delicious elegant morsels to serve with after-dinner coffee.

Well ahead of time, wash and dry
   1 punnet strawberries, with stalks on
Chill a large plate in freezer while melting in double boiler over simmering water
   100g cooking chocolate, broken up, with
   3 teaspoons butter
Stir to combine mixture and add gradually
   1-2 teaspoons water, *only just enough*
   to produce a thick dipping consistency
Pour into cup to give depth for dipping. Hold each strawberry top with tweezers, dip halfway into chocolate, then place carefully on chilled plate. Keep refrigerated until required.

ACKNOWLEDGMENTS

The time has come to say how grateful I am for the help I have received from the John Oxley Library in Brisbane, the State and Mitchell Libraries in Sydney, and Vintage Books in Toowoomba. But just as it is impossible to include every interesting old building in a book this size, there is not space enough to list all the books and papers that I read—only the most memorable.

Moreton Bay Couriers, 1846
History of the Colony of Queensland, William Coote, 1895
Tom Petrie's Reminiscences of Early Queensland, Constance Petrie, 1904.
In the Early Days, J.J. Knight, 1895
Jubilee History of Queensland, (ed.) E.J.T. Barton, 1919
Brisbane Courier Centenary Issues, 1923
Historical Miscellanea, J.H. McClurg, Royal Historical Society of Queensland, 1959
Brisbane Town in Convict Days, J.G. Steele, 1975
Life in the Cities, Michael Cannon, 1975.

I am also most grateful for the very special Queensland recipes kindly given to me for this book by:
Jill D'Arcy, Food Writer, The Courier Mail
Blair Edmonds, A.B.C., Brisbane
Dee Hall and Jan Massey
Coral McKillop, Home Economics Department, College of Catering and Hospitality Services, Coorparoo.

Measures without Misery

Most of us still wonder why our lives had to be complicated by metrics. Especially in the kitchen, where our ingredients come in grams and many of our recipes are in ounces.

The secret is not to worry, because almost all conversions can be approximate without any disastrous consequence to our cooking. The best example I can give you is that the ounce is converted into 30 grams in Australia, into 25 grams in England, we both multiply this by 16 to come up with 450 grams to the pound, and we accept that its official equivalent is 500 grams!

However, in order to keep our cool, we have to have some idea of what we are doing. And I find the following guide—which I worked out last year for the Sydney cook book—very handy for quick and easy reference; I hope you will too.

**Approved Australian Standard Measures,
using Metric Cups and Spoons.**
*Cup weights for solids are approximate only, as they vary according to ingredients.

1 teaspoon = 5g/5 ml   1 tablespoon = 4 teaspoons
    (But 1 USA tablespoon = 3 teaspoons)

1oz = 1½ tablespoons = 30g/30ml
2oz = ¼ cup = 60g/60ml
4oz = ½ cup = 125g/125ml
8oz = 1 cup = ½lb = 250g/250ml = ½ USA-European pint
10oz = 1¼ cups = 300g/300ml = ½ UK-Australian pint
16oz = 2 cups = 1lb = 500g/500ml = 1 USA-European pint
20oz = 2½ cups = 600g/600ml = 1 UK-Australian pint
1000g/1000ml = 1 kilogram/1 litre

Oven Conversions, Fahrenheit and Celsius.
275F = 140C 300F = 150C 325F = 160C 350F = 180C
375F = 190C 400F = 200C 425F = 220C 450F = 230C

Kitchen Utensils, Inches and Centimetres.
½" = 1¼cm   1" = 2½cm   8" = 20cm   9" = 23cm

Index

After the Main Course